YOUR

JOB SUCKS!

...Buy your freedom

by Dwight Droze

YOUR JOB SUCKS!

By Dwight Droze

 www.facebook.com/WhyJobsSuck

 @YrJobSucks (Twitter)

Published by Life Application Ministries
Publishing (LAMP)
P.O. Box 165
Mt. Aukum, CA 95656

Printer: createspace.com

INDEX

DEDICATION

This book was written for everyone who has a job and wants to change their financial situation for retirement.

The first step to change is understanding what the problem is; that is this book along with a little philosophy. Next is changing your philosophy of money and how retirement will be in the future. While in the philosophy stage the financial education really begins and helps to develop your strategy. The education will never end on your journey to the path of financial freedom.

It is also a tool for people who do personal finance seminars, multi-level marketing coaches, real estate agents, real estate and stock seminar professionals. A tool to remind those who are on the fence that it is time to take action on your future financial freedom.

This book is your slap in the face when it comes to jobs. Sometimes it's your only path back to reality. Because your job sucks and you know it.

THE OPENER

Let me start by telling you why you have this book in the first place, you are in one of these three categories. Reason one is you bought this book because your job sucks. Reason two is someone else knows your job sucks and bought it for you. Reason three is that the book is on clearance because it sucks and no one wanted it, but you got the clearance special because you're cheap.

Why are you so cheap? Because your pay sucks, which shows that it's all about the money. At that clearance price it became affordable to you because you assessed your risk and thought the clearance price was worth it to see if it relates to you and your crappy job. At which point it brings us back to number one because you wouldn't have bothered if it wasn't true.

Why any opinions from me? Well, I am not rich by any means or at least at the moment I am writing this. Assuming you have friends, tell them to buy this book and I may be on my way to riches. Better yet, just buy it for your loser friend because after all it is a great gift. (Note: you may be the loser friend that received this book.)

In fact, let me tell you how "un" rich I am by our society's standard. I drive a 1999.5 Jetta TDI with over 200,000 miles on it.

This baby gets over 50 miles per gallon with four people and a loaded down trunk on I-5 to San Diego from Lincoln, Ca. Ask me how I know.

My wife does have a newer car because I was tired of fixing her old beater Volvo. It wasn't cost effective as her car now is a VW Passat diesel and gets much better gas mileage. Do I keep the beater, or pay $180 a month to have a brand new car with a warranty, much bigger and that holds its value well? I take the latter. That payment is so cheap because of the amount we save on gas compared to her old car. Most cars, especially luxury cars when new are a financial death trap.

The only designer jeans I wear come from T.J. Maxx. RayBans are out of my league and at this time I don't even own a pair of sneakers. I'm a cowboy boot, work boot or flip flop type of guy anyway. I am also writing this on a hand-me down Mac Book Pro from 2010 while watching my fifty inch Walmart Black Friday two-hundred dollar TV.

We are working on down sizing to a 1,000 sq. ft. cabin on acreage we own that is off the grid as it will save us a ton of money. We have a nice log home we live in but the market is high and at the right price so its time to sell before it turns. In fact by doing this alone it will place $20,000 a year in our pocket after tax. Small sacrifices for a better future.

It is that time where investing in cash flow real estate is going to be a great opportunity in the areas I have been looking and we are preparing for it. We will touch on society's standards again later and why it is dangerous as most of society's picture of being "rich" is an extremely misguided fantasy.

I am also not a writer nor do I claim to be good at it. If it were a job I applied for I would suck at it and be fired immediately. I have to use this disclaimer here because if Taylor Swift is reading my book I want to prepare her for the lack of grammar war zone she is about to enter. For people like her my book might be a live grenade they feel obligated to dive on top of so the world is not exposed to my government education in English. For these types, you have been fairly warned if you lived long enough to make it to this paragraph.

Here is the truth. I am writing this book because my job sucks. And I am an expert at jobs that suck. You may not know it, but you probably are too. I just decided to find people who would pay me to read about why their job sucks. This is the moment when you realize you should have thought of it first.

Basically, I went around asking people why their jobs suck. Most of the time I get the same answers with some much longer than the others. I agree with many of the reasons in this book, but my number one is really near the end of this book and is my ultimate reason I feel jobs suck. This book in general is a different understanding on the general philosophy we are sold in school about getting a good job and going to college. I believe school teaches you how to be a good employee and not a business owner.

All joking aside I have learned a lot about investing in real estate, stocks, precious metals, business, history and the economics we live by. I have even flipped a condo and made nothing on it. I take that back. I got a $5,500 tax credit I had to pay back, bought precious metals with it and flipped them for a profit before I paid it back. We are in the process of flipping our home now for a nice profit if all goes well. This isn't the type of investing I am referring to as I don't believe capital gains is the way you should invest and it has a higher tax rate than cash flow since it's not passive income. Of course in our situation it is our primary residence so we won't have a capital gains tax.

I did invest in precious metals in September 2008 while it was near its lowest point before the market crashed because I knew ahead of time. It was just obvious after I had been trying to figure out where our economy was heading after almost three years. Pretty good eh? I just believed the right people and learned about the situation. I did try trading silver on margin in early 2008 which was a mistake as I didn't understand what I was doing and how a margin call worked. I lost a couple thousand dollars doing it but had time to recover from my expensive lesson.

I have been through real estate investing programs like Rich Dad and James Smith, along with owning many books on the subject including some on economics and the history of the FED. I've done multilevel marketing in ACN, Monavie, and some weird chewy vitamin with someone who ended up on The Bachelor. I shouldn't mention names because I'm not sure legally how it works, plus it was a very embarrassing for them I'm sure. Embarrassing or not the advertising for them was great so kudos for that matter.

Right now I am also playing with stocks and stock options which are very fun but again mostly for capital gains. I have a few friends who are great real estate investors and realize the benefits. What this all comes down to is I understand the philosophy of money and investing. I have ingrained it in my soul so much that you feel it and don't want it any other way because you can taste the financial freedom it offers.

To me, money is freedom at least from a financial perspective. To me a job is slavery, only because I have very high odds of knowing how the story ends financially. Now before my Christian buddies panic and scream "love of money" and only Jesus offers true security, I am strictly talking about your financial future here. Your financial security, as you are in the game right now whether you want to be or not. Also not to mention what's more evil; being kept in the dark and not understanding how money works, or knowing how to use it? Teach a man to fish right?

It is not so much a goal of mine to be rich in society's perspective because a goal to me is a limitation and their idea of rich in my opinion is wrong. It's the vision of real financial freedom and what it feels like to have that option. There are many like minded people out there searching for the same thing. This book is just a simple reminder you pop open from time to time to tell you "jobs suck" and to get out of the rat race to change your financial future. It is simple, and easy to read.

The Philosophy

Let's begin with a little philosophy that many of you may have heard of in passing, seminars, books, or even are on your way to success. First, we must ask what a "J. O. B." is. The short funny answer is just over broke. If you are honest with yourself a job is something you must do in order to pay your mortgage, rent, food, car payments, credit cards, utilities, etc. It's a JOB meaning that the day you stop working, it puts you and your family in a bad financial position.

You can measure your wealth by taking all of your expenses you have now, and see how long you can live that same lifestyle with the savings you have in cash and investments. You might only make it a week or a few months. You want it to be infinity, which is covering all of your expenses plus extra at a chosen lifestyle which comes from cash flow investments like real estate. In reality this is what being rich is.

How small of a percentage of your income can you live off at a lifestyle you want? I personally want to keep my expenses low enough and income high enough that I only need 1% of my income for my personal expenses.

You can only increase your income and decrease expenses. So if you have a plain old job and a huge raise isn't in the picture then focus on decreasing expenses and be real with yourself what is a true expense you need to have. That doesn't mean to go pay off your credit cards.

For example, lets say you have decent credit and have $15,000 in credit card debt. Your payment might not be very much even though you are paying a bunch of interest. So maybe you take the 15K you would pay off that card with and invest it in a property as a down payment that pays for that card in cash flow. So now someone else is paying that card off for you as well as a real asset which is your rental property and after the card is paid you continue to benefit from your past decision. This process should be used for buying a car as well. Buy a house that can pay for the payment on the car.

Just run the numbers and see where your

best option lies. Not to mention negotiation is something everyone is capable of. Call your credit card company and tell them you are considering balance transferring to another card unless they can lower your existing interest rate. You would be amazed how easy it is to save some money. Same goes for your cable provider. The retention department can always extend you a hand.

Some people say they love their jobs. I say that's a lie because they have to do it. Sure they chose which job they have but like a recovery program, you have to admit it to yourself before you can fix the problem. I don't really know how to explain it except they have to tell themselves that because they know they are not at the place they dream of or near retirement. Maybe they just can't visualize their retirement most are paying into.

Then you have the ones who say, "Oh, I will never retire. I like to work." Yet most of those people pay into a retirement as well, or are trying to find other ways to earn more money. If they love their job why do they bother with shooting for retirement? Because they ultimately want financial freedom, but deny the reality of their position when faced with opposition to their current retirement decisions. In reality, if their job disappeared tomorrow they would be in a horrible position.

I don't believe you can claim you love your job until it becomes an option to work. If you are a greeter at Walmart that has passive income from real estate, or portfolio income from royalties, stocks, or business that covers all of your bills plus more then it becomes an option to work. Once that is in place they can truly say they love their job and mean it. Now that's freedom.

The wealthy don't have jobs. Some of those wealthy people might disagree with me because they work 70 hours a week trying to grow their businesses and acquiring more wealth. The difference again is they could settle down, hire great management and take a back seat if they wanted to but they created the option to grow more wealth or scale back. I'm not talking about the small business owners that own a JOB. I'm talking bigger business. Most of us do not have that option yet and it's not the wealthy family's fault. Generally it is none but our own.

Whether you grew up in the ghetto, abused by your parents, or born in a barn means nothing. Money is not racist or above you. It is your slave if you use it right. And don't give me that inequality bull because the media claims some kids do not have access to good education. Our schools ranked 14th out of 40 according to the education firm Pearson on their overall index rank and score. (thelearningcurve.pearson.com).

PISA reports in 2012 the average reading literacy for students that were 15 years old ranked the US in the great place of 17th, 26th in math, and 20th in science (OECD.

org). The list goes on. I would say the entire US of A is screwed on public education. Now that is equality for you. Our government schools suck across the board so we are all equally worthless when it comes to education in our public schools. If this was American Idol we would have made it through Hollywood week, but we definitely aren't going on tour.

A college degree means nothing as well. Some of the wealthiest people in the world are high school and college drop outs. They obviously aren't stupid. Plenty of wealthy people have come from nothing. Some lost more money than the others through their journeys, but learned something about how money really works. And that is the answer. How to use money to make more money.

You must be like a bank. They don't even have anything to sell except storing your computer money and charging you for it. Then they loan out nine times your deposit thanks to fractional reserve banking and the FED to make a hefty return on nothing but your money and money they created. For them, DEBT equals MONEY. Using money to make money. This is where your future needs to be. Making money like a printing press.

One great explanation of this was on none other than Shark Tank. Kevin O'leary was explaining to a business owner that his business was broke and collapsing. He said, "I look at my money like soldiers. I send them to war and want them to take prisoners and bring them back. You send your money off to die."

Money and how it works is something most people will never understand. Mostly due to the lack of a real financial education and because they want instant gratification from that big TV, nice cars, second home, jewelry, high dollar clothing, and the newest cell phone. Not that you can't get a killer deal on those items. Just don't be fooled by the neighbor who seems to have nice things. Most likely they are broke, and lined with bad debt. I say bad debt because the wealthy are in millions if not billions of dollars of debt. Except, their debt makes them money. There's a big difference as mentioned above.

And don't be the guy who says doctors and lawyers are rich. They are just as strapped in debt as others are. For most people the more you make the more you spend. You can't make a poor man rich. You must change their philosophy and understanding of money.

People like to blame the wealthy for their problems and inequality. In reality, there may be a few elitists way up in the food chain that take advantage of situations but still there are very few wealthy people doing this. The 1% really do not matter in this equation. It's the 1% of the 1% you might ask how much power they have over government policies and things like this.

This is not a reason to make $15 per hour flipping a hamburger. Be real with yourself for a second. Do you really think you should make that much doing a job like that? If you do and I owned that business, I would make what is called a capital investment. I would eliminate your job with a computer because you now made it more cost effective to the company, plus no health insurance, employment insurance and less legal liability as well.

That work force of 20 people was just cut to 10 because of that wage increase. Sure those 10 people would be making $15 and hour if it were mandated but the question is, will one of them be you? McDonalds just did this with 7,000 automated ordering machines. Not to mention I have to keep those prices as low as possible so my broke consumers like you can afford it and I can beat my competitions price. You better show up with your "A" game and bring some value to your company because you are replaceable.

I remember listening to a radio show and he was playing things people said on the news about raising the wages to $15 per hour. I heard things like "we deserve nice cars and homes too" and "we deserve higher pay for our hard work." Are these people crazy? The answer to their position is right there. They want the nice stuff, and money for nothing. These are high school and college jobs and not for an adult with a family.

Unfortunately, our government has regulated and taxed businesses along with printing our cost of living into a hard place to survive and it has forced these providers into whatever job is available leaving these younger adults with no low paying jobs. Right now the Bureau of Labor Statistics is releasing job reports that shows the 55 and older group are taking the majority of the jobs and these jobs are almost all part time. What does that tell us? They can't afford to retire because the cost of living is going up and their retirement just isn't cutting it.

The under 24 age group is getting slaughtered. All of our high paying good jobs are being lost and the market is replacing lost jobs with twice as many part-time jobs so it looks as if the unemployment rate is going down when in reality you just work some crappy part time job because you have to. I can go on and on with this but I will spare you for now.

Let's sit back now and be realistic for a moment as I share 20 reasons why...

Your Job SUCKS!

Your Job Sucks!

#1

YOUR JOB DOESN'T EVEN WANT YOU TO HAVE YOUR JOB

It's the truth. There is someone in your company, or government agency that has the job to find a way to replace you with something more efficient and cost effective before you were even hired. And you had better be on time, because if you're not you are going to answer for it.

Got something else to do? Too bad. Because your company's profits depend on your sales, management, or service. So suck it up. Your personal time doesn't matter. You have enslaved yourself for a wage to someone else's demands and time is money.

You might say you have to have a job to make money off the start to then invest. This isn't always the case, but you are right that for most it is reality. No one said it had to be your money though. You can use other people's money through loans or even partnering after you put a deal together. But don't be offended when you read you have enslaved yourself. Just face the reality that you are a wage slave and accept it, then find the solutions.

The more bad debt you have that brings you no money is another form of enslavement. Even in the Bible it says you are slave to the lender. You MUST escape, and the only way is through investment, business, dividends, and royalties.

You can literally buy freedom by investing. Turn off your stupid XBOX and kittens on YouTube for a second and do something to make your financial situation better. Then you can pay yourself to eat chips and play video games. Remember, luck favors the prepared so get a real financial education and buy yourself some freedom.

Your Job Sucks!

#2

REQUIRES A COLLEGE DEGREE

Do you have your piece of paper yet? You know, that one you pay tens to hundreds of thousands of dollars for? Because those "high" paying jobs require it. Doesn't that suck? I don't have a degree. I can't sit through those horrible classes that have nothing to do with your career you are trying to get into. Not to mention everyone and their mom is getting a degree.

The supply is growing so fast that it is becoming worthless. I went to my wife's graduation and could not believe how many people got a degree in philosophy, political science and women studies. Really? What about business, financials, engineering, and science? No wonder we bring students from overseas. They study things that grow our capacity and make our lives easier, except they go back to their countries.

Don't worry if you can't pay for it right now. You can borrow money from your government and blow that student loan bubble even bigger before it pops. Or maybe they will just forgive the loan and make the rest of us pay for it. I mean send your debt to money heaven on a unicorn because that's where it goes right? Get real. As I write this 8% of those student loans are in default.

I went to college for real estate so I could get my license but it doesn't involve a degree of any sort. I took two classes online and real estate finance at Sierra College. This is where I learned about the coming crash the first time. I remember my teacher mentioning how interest rates have been low for so long that we could expect a crash. After I was done I went to take my state exam but I never studied. Those questions were way over my head and over most everybody's there. You needed a 70% to pass so I just guessed and surprisingly almost passed. I went again and guessed and almost passed again. I didn't even end up getting my license because I started meeting investors who told me it opens you up for potential lawsuits being a licensed professional. So I didn't bother until this year when I decided to list my house as all of my investment properties are planned outside of California anyway.

I took an economics class that was ridiculous as well. Keynesian economics has complicated things so much no wonder no one wants to take the class. You don't have to know most of that stuff to understand the economy. I will have a few books to read at the end of this book you might be interested in.

I took a stock investing class at the local college in 2011 as well which was actually pretty fun. It was ran by a teacher who also ran an investment office. I remember an older outspoken woman say her husband wanted to buy gold and silver because all of these commercials were on TV selling him on it. She continued talking saying how her brother was in the Navy and had invested in gold in the 80's when it hit $850 then he lost a bunch of money when it crashed. I couldn't take anymore when she said all these people are crazy for investing in that stuff. I said, "Well, I find it funny because you just said your retirement was down 40% but these people are crazy for investing in precious metals. I bought into precious metals in 2008 and am up 33% since the crash so I would say I'm doing 73% better than you are. Now who's crazy?"

I will put it this way. I would hire some computer nerd who has never seen a day of college over some college network "guru" who has some great degree that thinks they are worth a bunch of money because of that piece of paper. What does that tell you? Don't be a college nerd because of a piece of paper that says you accomplished handing tons of money over for a letter on another piece of paper. Hell, make a million bucks then buy a college degree from Yale for $800 and hang it on your wall. Then you can tell people you have an MBA. And when they ask you get to say, "Yea, Major Bank Account" and fly off in a helicopter. Your job can't do that can it?

I hated the education system! I am all for education but our government system is horrible. Everyone has to learn at the same pace. Unfortunately you must seek alternatives when it comes to financial education as our high schools just do not have this.

We have been programed to think that going to college is the "right thing to do". If you thought about it for a second you would realize how stupid that sounds. Maybe there is advertising involved in this, and profits for people. Ever think of that? Why not just take the classes you need or like to start a business? Or take a guitar class because you like music and skip all the advanced English.

There are some jobs where you want a professional with a degree. I guess I could make a good argument about a doctors education on practicing medicine instead of nutrition. I just don't want them practicing on me. Just put my leg back on when it comes off and I will stick to eating healthier.

"Stay in school" the celebrity says even though our schools systems rank horribly. Go to school, get a good job, and save for retirement. That's the plan your parents want you to have but it won't work this time around. I've got a better idea. Get a job or start a business, keep expenses low, invest the excess money in cash flow real estate, buy your freedom, and then do whatever you want. Just don't get stuck in the rat race trading your time for money working your whole life away at a job.

#3

WAKING UP AND BEING ON TIME

You know the best sleep is when you wake up and know you have to be somewhere you don't want to be and all you have to do is lay back down and say screw it. But your "Just Over Broke" requires your worthless body to show up on time or suffer the consequences. When your alarm goes off all you can think of is Twisted Sisters - We're Not Gonna Take It. This is one of the worst I have been told by anyone I ask.

Then there is the dreaded early wake up. When you roll over and look at the clock to add the hours up. "It's OK. I still have five hours to sleep" Then again and you're down to three. Next thing you know you are awake sitting there thinking you still have time and that nasty alarm beeping goes off. We have a one lane suspended wooden bridge over a river that I have to cross on the way to work. Sometimes I find myself in that daydream like you see in the movies where my teeth are clenched and I'm driving off that bridge. When I snap out of it I continue onto work.

I know waking up is a hard one for me even though I am rarely late. I refuse to hang out anymore at work than I have to. If I am not on the clock, there is no way I want to be there. I wouldn't blame someone who considers tying their shoes once the clock started or even going to the bathroom on the clock. I wasn't paid to drive there or home. Technically it's calculated in my pay and everyone's time is different.

One morning I even got hit by a car in my work parking lot while walking to my shop location. It's not like I wasn't paying attention. Like a laser guided missile, no matter which way I was going I knew the best route was on the hood so that's where I went. You know your job sucks when you get hit by cars. I've had many other close calls. I blew it too because all the old guys said I should have sued and milked that thing. They would have retired right then and there. Not that I was to proud to do it, but I wasn't hurt and I hit a bum on a bicycle before so it was fair. At least I gave him a dollar though.

I'm sure my coworkers all hate their jobs too and I wouldn't blame them. One even told a store clerk he would rather have his eyeballs plucked out by ravens than head off back to work. I just know every day I hear that alarm clock my day ends. By ends I mean I try not to even consider it a legitimate day until my next alarm goes off which is my clock out time. Yes, I have a timer on my phone for my clock out time, and my weekend start time.

I guess I'm just an old person ready to retire even though I'm only thirty. It's like in my mind I have worked a lifetime even though I haven't yet so I couldn't imagine another thirty plus years. I just have this ability to make it feel real when I think about it and I couldn't stand the idea of giving that much of my life away. You don't have to go down that long road to retirement. Make some investments and use it like magic to make that job disappear.

#4

NO TIME FOR FAMILY

Family time? I don't think so. Family Matters was a TV show and your job doesn't watch TV. You have to use the time you have after you've slept for eight hours, worked for nine plus, made dinner, and traveled to and from work before you can sit down and play with your kids. If you're lucky, you have your two days off.

With the cost of living rising due to inflation (the real definition of inflation being the expansion of the money supply and NOT rising prices which is the result of inflation), both parties of your family will most likely have to work. No longer can you work at McDonalds, pay your way through college, and pay rent. This isn't 1950 people.

No time for family adds to job creation numbers for the government. So when your wife or husband can't take care of the kids because it costs to much to live, just put your kid in that expensive day care so someone can have another job watching your child. Or put them in that public school as your baby sitter that you pay for through your taxes.

Unless of course you're in California where they are trying to put a bill through that your child can't even go to a private school without having all their state mandated vaccines. Yes, a private school you pay thousands for and your property tax is coming out to pay for other kids in public school. Not even a private religious school. Not even a day care!

I guess that leaves you with home school which means you have to quit your crappy job while one parent works and live in poverty. Either way, don't bother seeing them or anyone else you want to see until after you punch out on that time clock.

Luckily for the last few years that I have worked for the government I have been a seasonal employee. I'm permanent but only work 6-9 months a year before I'm laid off for the season. I get to see my son and get him out of day care. The sad part is day care is so expensive I actually make more money when I'm off. When I get laid off I like to call it a dry run retirement.

But in your situation it's really a drag. You have these kids and can't even see them. Think about it from a numbers perspective and add it up. Minus out your sleep, travel time, on the clock and lunch hours, then add up quality time you get to spend with your family. No wonder our divorce rate is so high and kids hate their parents. If you think waiting to have kids until you are financially successful is the smart thing to do, I've got bad news for you. The fed is printing so much money it will never feel like you are financially ready.

Don't worry, you have vacation time right? Oh we will get to that in number 11. But that costs money, and that brings us to number 5--you don't have any. Jobs can really eat away at your time with family but ends do have to meet. They just don't have to meet the way most people do it. Financial freedom. Buy it and go on a real vacation with your family.

#5

YOU DON'T MAKE ENOUGH MONEY

Of course you don't. No employee ever thinks they make enough. You will always be asking for a raise at a JOB. After all, if you had a better offer you would be there right? So face it, you take what you're worth in that position or be replaced by someone who will do it at that market price. I call it a wage slave. Trading your time to an employer for a wage.

Stop these government wage increases and let the market decide. Do you really think you are going to regulate yourself into a job? All you are doing is putting yourself out of a job if you're young and putting yourself in a crappy low paying part time job if you're older. Most old people coming back into the workforce are collecting social security so they don't want a full time job because there is a limit they can make before they start to be counter productive and lose money.

I can hear it coming. "But the corporations will pay us slave wages of a dollar an hour if we do that." First off, you already enslaved yourself by taking a job. Second, employers don't control wages, the market does. If someone can do it better and cheaper then they will fill the spot. I like that concept. You know why? That's what real capitalism is, when the market finds the price. Not crony capitalism where the government "creates" jobs through their inflation, manipulation, regulation and mandates.

Not to mention that company can become more competitive against other businesses and offer me a lower price on my goods and services I want to use. And if the competition wants to stay in business, they need to hire people like you that will trade their time for money and make it a better offer than the other company. Eventually you get a market price. What do you think happens in Silicon Valley at all the tech companies?

And don't overvalue yourself in a position unless you have data that matters to back you up. You are not crucial to the success of their business or special unless you are an exceptional salesman. But even salesmen are a dime a dozen.

A good friend of mine doesn't make enough money at his job but is an exceptional salesman. He knows he is worth more but is crippled by the fear of asking due to others falling to #5 at the owners decision to let them go for asking for a raise. The difference is he makes around 60% of what the entire branch location brings in over five or so other sales reps. Meaning everyone combined doesn't even bring in what he does. Now this is having your data advantage. As I am writing this book he has received a great raise because the CEO can see the benefit of his sales instead of him leaving to the competition.

Just know your numbers when you ask or bring a print out of them. If it's strictly customer service, good luck. You're a dime a dozen too and do not create money through sales though you might help retain a large percentage of it. So create value in yourself because there are an ever increasing number of people coming out of college you will compete with that have no jobs right now. Next time you find yourself asking for a raise, just remember you will never make enough at a job.

Let's leave #5 with an analogy. You just sat down at a restaurant and had the greatest burger of your life. I mean just incredible! Your bill comes, and it's $120 for your food and you need to change your diaper. All of a sudden you start to question your decision. "That burger was overcooked. It was dry, and I'm pretty sure that bun had mold on it" you say.

If that burger was $9.00 you would have told every friend you had (which you don't have because you're broke) that they had to eat there (except they're broke because their job sucks too). But what we found is that everyone has a price point where you cross that line of "it wasn't that good." This is like the job market.

If you work for a company at $10 per hour and are fairly productive then you are just like a good $9 burger to that company or entity. All of a sudden you sit your boss down and say I need a raise to $15 per hour and its like getting that $120 bill. Now your boss questions himself and says, "Well, they aren't that productive or crucial to my business."

You might get $11 per hour but you are pushing your luck any higher than that except in cases above.

Keep this in mind because this is how prices work. This is the process with negotiation or purchasing products as well. You gauge how much that TV is worth to you compared to the amount of dollars you are trading for it. Lesson learned. Repeat after me. I will never make enough money at a job. Now lets talk about some of those people that drive you nuts at work.

#6

THE PEOPLE YOU WORK WITH

It doesn't seem to matter where you go. You just can't escape those people you can't stand. Even if you leave and get another job, there you will find them again in another body. Your boss sucks. The owner sucks. Your mayor sucks. Even the president sucks. On top of that you're reminded of #5-- your pay sucks.

It's crazy that we just happen to stay or find ourselves at another place with more people that clash with our personalities yet we hang on because we have to make that money for ends to meet. Isn't that ridiculous? Just one more reason to create something great and start investing.

I know this is a big one. I have had some supervisors that were in love with the so called "power" they had. Boy, in my mind sometimes I was Macho Man Randy Savage laying the law down for corrupt supervisors. Then there is the gossip. This one really drives me to madness. Do they really care that much to complain about people behind their backs? I mean that person might be a piece of trash but I try not to even remember my day at work in the first place because it just would remind me where my future was heading. Please if you ever work with me at a job, don't feel bad if I don't remember you.

Just remember, it doesn't matter where you go because you will meet again. And don't stay because you like working with a few of the people there. Let them stay working with those types of people while you work on freedom. Go buy your freedom and escape from the sea of idiots you can't stand to be around. This may include family.

Your Job Sucks!

#7

TAXES FROM EARNED INCOME

Taxes suck, all around. The old saying of taxes and death are true. And thank Roosevelt and the signing of the Current Tax Holding Act of 1943, when your income comes from a job you pay taxes first before you get to feed your family. Why? Because the tax code doesn't want you to have a job!

The tax code wants you to have a business, and investments, especially in cash flow real estate. The tax system is geared towards it and for a good reason. Because you create jobs and growth with business and investment. The more you save on taxes, the more you invest into growth. We still have the highest corporate tax rates in the world and those need to be cut. People would love to have the rich pay more in taxes but you know what I say? Why don't we all have a major tax cut?

People think they're patriotic by paying income taxes but I've got news for them. Income tax didn't exist in this country except in the civil war and not again until 1913! That's right people. The IRS was created in 1913, the same time the Federal Reserve was to take your money and pay back the Federal Reserve Bank for loaning the currency your government is printing. Yea, read that again. Scam? You betcha. Being patriotic would mean no income tax on earned income from a job.

If you knew anything other than your job you would know that we shut down three other central banks in this country's history for robbing the people through inflation. And let's be clear again, inflation of the currency supply like the definition always was before approximately 1991 when it was changed to imply inflation was the rising of prices on goods and services. Talk about treating the symptoms.

Inflation is a stealth tax. It is printed into existence and the first person to spend it is in the best position because everyday the currency supply is expanded your currency buys you less. Your pay seemingly sucks because it cannot keep up with the symptom of inflation which is the rising prices. Basically more dollars chasing the same amount of goods.

Why don't you pay twenty-five cents for gas anymore? I mean, technology is better and should increase productivity which in return brings us lower prices right? Why is gas over three dollars a gallon where I live? Opec isn't driving the prices up. It is inflation and those barrels of oil are priced in dollars because we are the reserve currency of the world. Let me put that another way. The US dollar is the "gold standard" backing other currencies.

There is no gold backing your currency as Nixon took us off that in 1971 so we didn't have to give other countries our gold we said they could redeem their dollars for. We really screwed them. The last president to try keeping us on a gold standard was murdered and that was JFK. Remember the silver and gold certificates in the 1960s? Your dollars were redeemable in gold or silver at a bank just like we told the other countries they could do when we sold them our debt.

Today it says Federal Reserve "Note" which is a debt instrument. It is the same concept as holding a note (mortgage) on a home like a bank does when they loan you money to buy a home except the bank has a real asset (your home) while the currency is just the idea it is worth something because the government says you have to pay your income taxes with it. All kinds of things have been used as currency. I believe the longest lasting currency in the world was a stick. That's right a stick. Look it up with your gizmo.

Price deflation is your friend. You may hear the talking heads speaking negatively about it on the news but let's look at a brief concept. When you hear "we need prices to rise" they are saying we want consumers to have to spend more money. Now I don't know about you but I think I spend enough on gas, food, and all other living expenses already. Look at TV's, computers, and cell phones. They are a perfect example of price deflation as technology has gotten better.

Did you know gas is still twenty-five cents if you price it in silver? That's right. Silver quarters from the 60's are worth over three dollars in metal value alone! Now that is storing value. Why do you think the government has removed it from circulation in your coins? Because the metal costs more than the face value of the coin.

This is what Athens did way back when and had their inflation event. They devalued their coins with copper until the gold was thinned out and they made so many coins (expanding the currency supply) that there was hardly any gold in the money. Everyone had some so no one wanted it for goods. It always went back to gold.

This is all very brief but you can dig deeper on the subject if you study things like money's history and Austrian economics. For the most part they only teach Keynesian economics now in our schools. They are all theories that basically teach that the government grows economies through inflation and people have to spend instead of save for investments to retire. Works out great for governments but not the people. A great book is called How an Economy Grows and Why It Crashes by Peter Schiff and a great cartoon video is called The American Dream on YouTube.

Deflation of a currency supply is where it hurts. This was like the great depression. The FED can literally cause a depression or the business cycle. When jobs and businesses grow because there is a misallocation of resources (money flying everywhere it wouldn't be in a normal market) then businesses and jobs pop up that wouldn't have been there in the first place or maybe an entire industry.

When the money or credit supply is contracted (deflated) all that growth comes crashing back to reality and the market has to find which jobs and businesses are crucial at the time to their lives. Unfortunately, it hurts really badly but that's the consequences of a central bank and fiat currencies.

Let's look at some quotes from some of our fore-fathers:

Thomas Jefferson

Lets look at a couple quotes from Thomas Jefferson to start:

"If the American people ever allow private banks to control the issue of their currency, first by inflation, then by deflation, the banks and corporations that will grow up around them will deprive the people of all property until their children wake up homeless on the continent their Fathers conquered."

"I believe that banking institutions are more dangerous to our liberties than standing armies."

President Lincoln

"The Government should create, issue, and circulate all the currency and credits needed to satisfy the spending power of the Government and the buying power of consumers. By the adoption of these principles, the taxpay-

ers will be saved immense sums of interest. Money will cease to be master and become the servant of humanity."

Woodrow Wilson

What about the president that signed the federal reserve into law? What did Woodrow Wilson say in the end?

"I am a most unhappy man. I have unwittingly ruined my country. A great industrial nation is controlled by its system of credit. Our system of credit is concentrated. The growth of the nation, therefore, and all our activities are in the hands of a few men. We have come to be one of the worst ruled, one of the most completely controlled and dominated Governments in the civilized world no longer a Government by free opinion, no longer a Government by conviction and the vote of the majority, but a Government by the opinion and duress of a small group of dominant men."

You know what the bankers have to say about this? Let's see their famous quotes.

Bankers

The few who understand the system, will either be so interested from its profits or so dependent on its favors, that there will be no opposition from that class." ... "Let me issue and control a nation's money and I care not who writes the laws." —Mayer Amschel Bauer Rothschild, 1744-1812

"The bank hath benefit of interest on all moneys which it creates out of nothing." –William Paterson, founder of the Bank of England, 1694

There are tons of these quotes from major historic figures throughout our world history. So remember, your taxes aren't for the government but for the federal reserve for "loaning" our government its own currency at interest. That's why we have to forever grow our debt because it is impossible to pay off. If you create a currency and loan it out but require double back (interest), where are they going to get the other half? Well, they can borrow more from you!

That's how it works and why our system will collapse. It's a fiat currency, meaning backed by nothing. There isn't one currency in the history of the world that has lasted as a fiat currency. Every single one has failed and went to zero. To understand income tax, you must understand our monetary system. Taxes suck no matter what kind they are, but it's much worse when it's earned income from a job.

#8

SOCIAL SECURITY

Yeah, you know what I'm talking about if you're between ages 20-45. You're paying for the living of people who sold your future and lined it with trillions of government debt that you have to pay back! And even worse, you won't ever get your money! The government is broke. Why do you think they have to borrow from China and the FED? You can kiss your Social Security goodbye.

Sure your parents or grand parents might be collecting it. But it's broke. Who says they can't keep raising the age you can collect it? What if by that time you have to be 72 to collect it? What if you never make it there? Too bad. They benefit by you kicking the can because they get to pay it to someone else.

In 1999 the Office for Management and Budget said that the fund's assets:

"Do not consist of real economic assets that can be drawn down in the future to fund benefits. Instead, they are claims on the Treasury that, when redeemed, will have to be financed by either raising taxes, borrowing from the public, or reducing benefits or other expenditures. The existence of large trust fund balances, therefore, does not, by itself, have any impact on the government's ability to pay benefits." —Office of Management and Budget 1999

In other words they are a bunch of IOU's from the government and if the fund runs dry they can just print all the money to pay you (bailouts) which in return we pay taxes for the borrowed money. The people who receive the monies can't buy much because they just massively inflated the currency supply (inflation), and now your prices are going to rise dramatically so your purchasing power was just eroded. This is why fixed incomes suck. Because inflation produced by the FED is your enemy.

The Merriam-Webster dictionary defines a pyramid scheme as "a usually illegal operation in which participants pay to join and profit mainly from payments made by subsequent participants." Turn away! Nothing to see here. But don't worry, the government makes the rules so everything is going to be OK.

My dad collected social security for some years because of his back from being a mechanic. Let me tell you, we were broke. Lived in a house made of asbestos tile and a floor you could set a marble on and watch it roll to the other side. It was an older fire station barracks in Lincoln, Ca. It's now a parking lot as the city was going to use eminent domain to provide a use for the public by bulldozing our house.

Don't let them trick you into waiting until you're older to collect a higher payment either. Take it early on because you might as well get some and the amount you are forfeiting over the years you wait is a lot of money when you're about to die anyway.

So keep eating that GMO science experiment food and drinking that fluoride water because I have some money to collect that I've paid into. And as long as you're still kicking around, I may not get mine.

#9

YOUR RETIRE-MENT WILL SUCK

Face it. Most of you saving for retirement are handing your money to some investment group that sold your company on why you should use them. Talk about trust! Back to my Christian buddies here. This is what we call gambling right? Blindly handing money over hoping on some great return. Pick fund "A" for riskier investments or fund "G" for conservative.

As you think you're retiring, they have raped your fund dry from fees, and more. Welcome to the world of mutual funds. Not to mention when the market crashes, none of those people seem to ever have it right. You know why? Because they SUCK at their jobs. Even worse, it's with your money! So you can forget about retiring. Your retirement will most likely suck.

In a mutual fund you put up money, take all the risk, and benefit from probably 20% of the profit. Most of these places are forced to invest the way their organization wants them to. Your guy might be really good in his personal portfolio but unfortunately they aren't allowed to deviate from the path that their corporation demands.

And diversify? Let's break this down because it is a load of bull. By diversifying your portfolio they mean have money in multiple different industries incase one industry has a big drop on stocks, the other industry may have a big rise bringing you no or a small loss. They forgot to mention that also brings you a small gain or no gain at all! That advice is for the people who go to work, hand over their money to a company, and go to sleep. I wonder how many people were diversified when the market tanked and took at huge loss? Remember all those people who were down 40-60%? You may have been one of them. Time for a new broker and time to learn a little on your own.

Wouldn't it be much easier to have passive income from real estate and other sources? You even have your own business structure that works to your advantage for taxes and the freedom to get paid while you are on vacation for three months. Now that's retirement and most likely a very early retirement if you are young and good with your money.

Use this example. Take $10,000 and use it for a down payment on a property that costs $50,000. That property might only bring $200 a month net but that's a 24% cash on cash return a year and after you get all your money back in four years its return becomes infinity. Not to mention you never even made a payment on the house. Someone paid it off for you. And why sell it? You can just pull out equity in small amounts to make sure you still have cash flow and use that money for new properties tax free. You can't tax that type of debt. You can even buy rental properties with a self directed IRA and the cash flow grows tax-free. There are so many strategies it's an unfair advantage you can have over your average person.

Now let's look at a 401k and make a realistic example. By far the majority of people do not contribute much to their retirement in the first place. And you are told to put in the minimum if your employer pays a match. Let's do this. You make $40,000 a year, give 5% as your contribution, and have a 1% salary raise a year. You are 30 years old, and want to retire at 60. Your annual rate of return is 5% a year over those 30 years. You will contribute $70,265 over 30 years and with your employer match at 50% they contribute $35,133. Including all of your interest you have $229,054 after 30 years. That is a joke my friend. That doesn't even include the FED's bogus inflation rate.

Go back to the rental property example now and lets go deeper. Lets assume you don't even raise your rents with inflation since the FED claims there isn't any. Just that $200 per month coming in is $72,000 after 30 years but you didn't have to wait until you were almost dead to use it and pay a penalty for pulling it out before a certain age. Again that property could be paid off by then which would mean your cash flow increased dramatically if not almost doubled. I didn't even calculate that into this equation. So assuming the house didn't increase in value you can add that $50,000 property to you $72,000. Also that $70,000 you would have saved for your 401k is in your pocket and could have been a down payment on seven other properties.

Now this is where it gets dramatic. You forgot that you didn't have to wait to collect your money since it's not a 401k and over-time you get $10,000 saved from cash flow you buy another house and collect another $200 per month. You could have repeated that seven times from cash flow and seven from your savings of 5% of your paycheck a year by that 30 years bringing you to a nice little cash cow. And don't forget this is still assuming none of those properties are paid off after thirty years. Like Monopoly, you want green houses and red hotels.

Even if you started that 401k at 18 years old you would be destroyed by someone who started real estate investing at the same age from the example above. By the way, your tax rate with that 401k will be whatever the income tax rate is in the future and we know taxes are rising. With real estate you get to depreciate your rental property over twenty-seven and a half years against the income it produces.

So eat that giant loss and hunker down at that 9 to 5 for the "long term" because you have to make it all back before you "retire" and that clock never stops ticking.

Your Job Sucks!

#10

THAT GOVERN- MENT PENSION

Like social security, most of you younger folks paying into a pension will probably never see it. As the generation before you burns through your money on new TV's and health care, you will be caught holding the bag. Especially government pensions. Like #8, they're broke. So use it while you can if you're on it because you just enslaved the generation after you.

Congratulations, little Johnny's future looks grim. Why? You are claiming the income on future generations with a pension. So unless there are more workers funding the pension before the last generation, or they are far more productive with less people, then that pension is dead. That's the reality.

I won't pay into a pension (if it's an option) at my age because the odds are it wont exist when I'm in my 60's or I will be paid with an inflated currency and a cup of black coffee will be twelve dollars. "Coffee twelve dollars" you say? NO WAY! Yes way you blind government teat milker. You don't pay five cents for a candy bar anymore right? It's almost a dollar at Walmart now. That's a 2000% increase. Your coffee was around a 1000%.

"But I work for the state of California so I have a great pension plan." That's what they say. Well, don't be surprised when California is the first state to be bailed out because your pension isn't really there. I guess we don't call them pyramid schemes when it's the government.

Test. What if the economy has a major down turn again and there are more people on pensions then those working? Again your retirement is dead in the water. Do you think your pensions are paid with unicorn bucks? That's a bad example because technically I would consider the US dollar unicorn currency. But you get the concept. Even dividends have major cuts in these downturns when you're trying to live off them.

I was on the phone with Calpers (CA State pension) trying to cash out some money I have in there and asked a few questions. The guy tried to remind me that I get a 6% return on my money and generally with all the benefits I will probably get to draw on ten times the amount I actually pay in. Did you catch that? Obviously we can't all do that or the fund breaks. If I had a company that made this claim I would probably be in jail.

And 6%? I just made 40% on a stock option yesterday. I'm up 50% on a rare minerals mining company right now in three weeks. Mark my words, your pension sucks and you can add that to your job that does too.

Your Job Sucks!

#11

VACATION TIME SUCKS

That doesn't seem right does it? But it's true! Two weeks of vacation a year? That is some kind of sick joke. Have you ever turned in that leave request form to your supervisor just to find out there is a project or someone else taking a vacation at the same time you wanted to spend time with your family? Ouch.

Sure you can store up some of that vacation time but there are also limits at each place of how much and how long before you need to take it. In other countries like Australia people leave for at least four weeks on vacation. That's a little better but wouldn't you like to be in control over that area of your life? I know I do and that's why you need to invest in things that bring passive income. A job will never provide that type of freedom for you and I know because I'm a crappy job expert.

I almost forgot you have dogs, cats, hamsters, and a chinchilla you have to take care of somehow while you're gone on your pathetic two week vacation. Your garden is dying when you come back so you have to pump it full of miracle grow. The house is falling apart because a water main broke (just happened to me), and someone left the heater on so your bill is outrageous.

This wouldn't be so much of a problem but your pay sucks because your job sucks so you can't afford that vacation to begin with and pile the rest on your credit card so you can pay it back later. I guess you could get no vacation time, but I feel like that little time they give you is a punch in the face. You need to exit the job market if you want more than this.

Vacations should be enjoyed like your job doesn't exist and there is nothing to worry about. Unfortunately most of us take that vacation and are checking emails, contacted by coworkers or clients and worry about a project that is due or something along those lines. That job just seeps its ugly face into every crack of your worthless vacation it can.

Hawaii was great this year. It was actually hard to leave the last time I went but then I catch all those broke people who were thinking the same thing. I didn't want to make bracelets with sea shells and the hair off my back to sell on the street corners while I look like a fifty year old burned cow hide. I'm just kidding, I don't have hair on my back. But seriously, they do sell those on the streets. They did create their own business I guess but it's not a big enough production run and that will be in number 12.

Your vacation sucks already as it is because you are penny pinching and staying in a hostel. If you had your investments lined with passive income you wouldn't be worried about it. In fact, it may be a business expense. Let's be real though. Your job doesn't care if you live, die or grow mushrooms in your crack. Pucker up and kiss your vacation life goodbye because jobs suck.

#12

SMALL BUSINESS... A JOB YOU OWN

Do you know why this is in here? Because the wealthy know when you own a true small business, you own a job! Sure, you might be at the top of the food chain on your shareholder list, but you have to be at work and run the show. That title sounds great though right? President and CEO of worst job USA. And when reality comes crashing down and you file for bankruptcy, you will remember that not only do jobs suck but sometimes owning one is even worse.

Making the right investment decisions and investment education makes you rich. Rich people have a choice because they created that option and boy do I love options.

I'm not saying a small business is bad. I'm just saying when you have to be there every-day and your money is on the line, things can get very stressful. If that business goes down you don't just lose your job you lose your life's work, savings and generally no unemployment insurance either.

All businesses start small but most fail by their fifth year. Many successful people have had forty businesses before they landed a very successful one. Not that this should discourage you, just don't lie to yourself and think your knitting skills are going to take you to the big time unless the big time is a loss in your bank account and credit score.

Don't take offense to this because you own a small business and you think you love your "business" which I would most likely call a job. Just face the facts. If something happened at your company or the economy crashed you could be destroyed and back at square one in no time. There is no safety in your position. While you are in it you might be making better money from a nominal perspective so start investing that and sell the business for a profit if the chance arises or collect a royalty on your product.

If it's in multi-level marketing or whatever new names they use for them, these can be a very cheap way to start and learn to sell. You can make a lot of money doing these businesses and use it to fund your investments so that one day you can retire early and enjoy your life. I know they aren't all the same and offer many different choices, from services to products, and some may not be a good business model. Don't let someone tell you they are scams and be aware that they are hard work if you really want to make it somewhere.

I hope you are not the person who has this great business or idea that is really worthless and mortgages their house to keep the business running. I thought I had the greatest invention of all time. I called it the "boob tube" as it was a breast feeding device for babies that a mother could use from a distance while she was in the car next to the baby. I got the idea after my wife was trying to feed the baby in the back seat. Could it solve a problem? Sure I guess. Now if someone uses my idea and makes millions then I guess they did it better. It was the best bad idea I had so give me a break.

Now has mortgaging a house for a business worked before? Sure it has. But this isn't the Hunger Games and the odds aren't in your favor so find a time to cut any losses and run. A lot of small businesses are a titanic with no life boats. Be passionate but know when to run like hell.

Bishop Francis Browne knew to leave the Titanic when he got a memo that said, "Get off that ship." Today his pictures are some of the only ones that left that ship at its last port stop. Weird, I know. There are some convincing conspiracy theories on it as I'm sure you will come up with the same in order to justify your business.

I know someone who told me they want to pass on their business to be run by family and sit back to collect 30% of the profits as a retirement. I don't think they realize a smart business owner wouldn't work for seventy cents on the dollar when they can just start the same company themselves and take 100%.

When I was nine years old I came up with my first business. I lived in Lincoln, CA next door to the police and fire station. Behind us was an alley that led to the popular small grocery store on 5th street called Photos Market. One day strolling through the alley I noticed next to the dumpster a few heavy large stacks of brand new newspapers still in their factory banding.

It hit me instantly. People buy news papers! I can stand in front of the store and sell them before they buy one in the store and if they forgot to I can remind them on their way out. After all I was only selling them for market value of fifty cents. I sold those babies like crazy in my mind. In reality I only made about $2.50 but in a very short amount of time. People were eating up the idea of a little boy bringing them back to the days where they passed them out in the streets whether they bought one or not.

Little did I know, my business was about to crash. A man noticed that I sold him a paper that was over a week old and when he came out of the store he had no problem telling me. He didn't ask for his money back that I remember but I had to take those newspapers and put them back by the dumpster in the alley. For the short time I was there, it was far more than I would have made mowing a lawn and a lot less work. The problem was that there was no residual income along with the fact that I was selling last week's news. The papers didn't pay me each time someone read it even after I sold it. I realize today that you need to make money by the second with our technology to make it big.

Later when I was about eleven I had another idea. It was all about Christmas in our town as they had a big parade that ran near our house every year. People lined the streets and there was a big festival with food, singing, and carriage rides. We had this big oak tree out back by the alley that spewed out tons of mistletoe and it hit me again. People buy mistletoe around Christmas! At least I saw it in the movies.

I climbed up that tree and cut down two big branches of it then cut them into smaller branches. I went in the house and took a bunch of sandwich bags and packed them with the mistletoe. When nighttime came 5th street was filled with people and it was time for my operation to start.

I went to the corner of 5th and F Street where there is a small Chinese restaurant now. I sold a bunch of those bags at two dollars each. I didn't have anything left to sell. It was probably around twenty dollars but that was a lot to me. Even at that age I couldn't believe people would buy this fungus to kiss under when you could get it for free. Again I didn't realize I had owned a job. Once the product was out or people didn't want to buy what I was offering anymore my business was over. It was time to take it behind the barn and shoot it.

Another thing I did was pan-handle at school. I went to Glen Edwards Middle School in Lincoln, Ca. Friends thought it was funny when I walked around with a can asking for change and people would give it to me including friends. I only did it a handful of times but I was on the reduced lunch program so having any money was great because I could use it on whatever I wanted.

Sometimes when I walked home I would stop by Bills Frosty get an ice cream.

I had to sell myself on this one and didn't even need a product. It was like being a street performer in a city of people my age. Not that it made me popular, because it didn't. I still was good at football so it saved my reputation but was uncool and had a bowl cut, which didn't impress the ladies let me tell you.

Owning a job isn't always bad but be realistic and plan for the future while you're ahead. Time is marching on and you will find out sooner or later that the financial musical chairs are about to leave you with no place to sit. Don't get caught owning a job.

Your Job Sucks!

#13

LUNCH BREAK

The only good thing about it is you get to stop doing your job for thirty minutes to an hour. But if you look at the big picture, you're just extending the time you get to stay before you leave that god forsaken place to go home and try to accomplish something that needs to be done. Not to mention for most jobs you're not even paid to stay that extra time even though you are away from home and your family. What a horrible thing to do!

When I was a fire fighter in the US Forest Service we were paid for sixteen hours on the fires, then went to a spike camp to eat some chum thrown in five gallon bucket a helicopter might fly or a truck drive in and sleep far away from our families while not getting paid. County and state fire fighters were paid twenty-four hours a day but not us.

I made $12.79 an hour to work like a slave digging fire line and hauling brush for hours on end. Running and hiking for miles and miles everyday, then going to emergency calls, talk about under paid. Two of us were vegetarians and boy we weren't prepared for our government lunches. Michelle needs to get on that.

One day we had a bagel in our sack lunch. Just a bagel, that's right. All those taxes were really helping us out there. Then I went to the Hot Shots which is basically the special forces of fire fighting. I was seasonal so was about to be laid off anyway until next season. Being a fire fighter in the Forest Service really makes you hate hiking. Now do you think you should make $15/hr. flipping a hamburger? With the real inflation number you probably should but the FED doesn't care about that.

Now look down at your GMO, bleached, white, enriched bread that surrounds your government spam and ask yourself why you do what you do and be honest. You do it to pay the bills. Now start paying yourself first and invest.

Forget the garbage you buy that you claim you need. You need a life while you're on this planet so you might as well enjoy it before they tax the air you breathe or you're dead. And you won't do that by taking a two week vacation a year. As long as your management approves a vacation that is.

Your lunch break is bitter sweet but should remind you where you are, where your future is, and where you should be.

#14

THE HOT GIRL AT WORK

This is bad. I think every guy experiences this at some point. You don't have a chance of landing her or at least keeping her. You know why? Because she knows your job sucks! She knows your pay sucks, your benefits suck, and you're going nowhere fast. Why? Because her job sucks and she works with you! You are guilty by association. I'm not saying good guys finish last. I'm saying guys with crappy jobs do.

Age does come into play here so I will give you that if you are twenty-two or younger. But if you are thirty and working at the Mc-Donalds drive through you had better have a good story. I know right now the job market sucks in general but I think you know what I'm saying. People aren't impressed, and not that it matters, but it does.

You're going to break the bank trying to impress her with tacos at the local Mexican restaurant. And you know why she went with you there? Because she was smarter and figured she would break your bank instead of hers because her pay sucks too! I don't blame her. Look at yourself. Now look at her. That's about as far as it goes. Get over it and get a real financial education or pay for an expensive education and make all the mistakes on your own.`

All I'm saying is she is out of your league and your job isn't giving you any upper hand. Society has been brainwashed to think success is being a doctor, lawyer, engineer, scientist, professor, and pilot. What do all of those still say? SUCCESS right? OK I will give you the pilot back because it used to be cool to be an airline pilot. Kind of like the construction worker in the YMCA songs. Now girls just make fun of us when they drive by. Why do we think this way? Again we are told that's what success is by an aging population that is broke.

Trust me I have been there myself with my girlfriend's parents. They wanted her to marry a doctor or someone professional because she would be better off financially. Well, I've got news for them. I will actually have a retirement in the long run and they won't. Don't be a fool. Get your finances and education started on the right track and start investing because that hot girl is smarter than you and has already figured it out.

#15

IT'S LIKE GROUND HOG DAY

EVERY single DAY is the same! You get there, it's the same people, desk, office, boss, and pay. Like in the movie Inception, sometimes you need to have a special token or item that no one else could possibly have just to make sure it's not a bad dream that you are lost in.

Some people worry about sleep paralysis, but I worry about being in a coma with an everlasting dream of a day at work. It's like that dream where you know you can run fast but like the beginning of Forest Gump and you can't get your miracle legs working yet. Few jobs offer an exciting change daily next to police, fire, and some military.

Can you imagine working in a call center, customer service, or for an agency doing collections? It's not just the people you work with there, it's also the crazy customers who want only blue M&M's. It's really a drag when you realize your financial future is not advancing and this job or one like it is the way life will be for the next thirty plus years if you don't do something about it.

If you're eighteen think about it this way. Your retirement starts 47 years from now (if you're lucky) and that job at McDonalds is most likely similar to what the majority of you will be doing your whole life. Maybe it's a furniture store, car salesman or working at Walmart. Who knows, but its a long way off.

This number really drives home the idea of my coworker who would rather have his eyeballs plucked out by ravens.

Groundhog Day is referring back to the movie. If you haven't seen it, please do and make sure you look at it in the light of a job.

Your Job Sucks!

#16

INCON-
VENIENCE

Jobs are an inconvenience. They don't pay you for your help. They pay you for your time because you are trading your time for currency at different rates. So we can say you are paid for the inconvenience of having to drive and stay at such a dreadful place.

You always have an appointment for something on a work day or something more important to be accomplishing but your stuck at that J. O. B. (just over broke) forever or at least until you reach that area of success where your cash flow from real estate, stocks, or royalties are greater than your daily expenses.

Until this is met, this inconvenience will eat you alive by melting your time away. Just add up the numbers. You only have twenty-four hours in a day and nine plus is spent driving, working, and eating before you do anything else for your day. That's over one-third of your time plus sleep, eating dinner, breakfast, groceries, etc. You get that tiny sliver of time to your family. It makes sense though right? Someone has to work those jobs, but the beauty of it is that it doesn't have to be you.

The worst is when your car breaks down. Any money you have saved was planned for something else and maybe a different type of emergency. Now you have to get to work but you need to fork out $1,000 plus to fix your heap of a car. It's even harder when you are so broke you have to fix it yourself and time is counting down before work the next day. My last job I didn't get paid sick time, vacation, or holiday so this is a bad deal for me. In fact we had a huge fire coming toward our house so I had to take a few days off while everyone was evacuated so I could run my chain saw clearing brush and falling trees from the house. My friend and I even had to hide from the sheriff deputy telling everyone to leave the area. I wasn't even paid. Talk about an inconvenience. You better believe we raised our insurance though. It missed by a mile, literally, and we listed our home for sale shortly after to flip for a profit.

If you didn't have to be at work the car issue wouldn't be such a big deal. Especially if you had the money even if it was planned for another investment. It may even be a corporate expense you get to use pretax money on if you had a business that held your real estate or another type of business. We know there are many other issues we can call an inconvenience but I think we get the point. Jobs are in your way of the freedom you long for.

Your Job Sucks!

#17

RICH PEOPLE DON'T HAVE JOBS

Rich people have an option. Sure you think celebrities work and they do. It's just that they make a ton of money doing something they "love" and if they invest it properly then they can make that claim because they can take those millions and buy real estate to create some nice cash flow. Notice I said celebrities? Not the starving musician or actor that hasn't made it anywhere. They have a job. It really sucks to be in that position even though it is part of the journey.

You will never be rich or wealthy working solely a job and not moving your money into something that has passive income. You should take the excess you save and invest. I'm just stating if you don't do at least that much then don't count on financial freedom because you're a modern day wage slave and you're choosing that each and every day you make a decision not to increase your financial education. The rich can work sixty plus hours a week if they please and work hard. But its still an option for them.

Rich and wealthy people get it. Well, I guess not all rich people as many NBA and NFL players blow it when their career is over. Did you ever hear of MC Hammer? Same type of deal. You can't make a poor man rich. By poor I mean poor in financial education and poor spending habits. You can be rich nominally but be poor with all that money. It's like when people win the lottery and go buy that big house then can't afford the taxes in the future. They get a Ferrari and can't replace the brakes that cost $15,000. These aren't really rich people in my mind. Sure they make a ton of money from sports, CD, and DVD's, but they don't sell forever so they lose it all once their ride is over. Royalties from those things are great but you better be moving that cash flow into something like real estate. You want to be rich in cash flow from efforts you made in the past. This is what the real rich and wealthy people do. So you don't have to be rich by society's idea but by cash flow that covers your expenses. That is being rich.

DO NOT use this excuse, here it comes… "I can never retire because I have to be doing something." I HATE THAT! No, you can never retire because you will be a broke, wage slave. You know what you'll be doing when you retire? Something you want to do! So you are doing something. Start a business you enjoy or are interested in. Go on mission trips or start a non-profit and give your time for what you love.

That excuse kills me. It's the easy way out. What happens if you get into a car accident and your neck is messed up for the rest of your life? Throws a wrench in that whole plan doesn't it? Generally that person is still paying into a 401k so they are lying to themselves. You don't think they would buy that winning lotto ticket off you? They want to retire just like everyone else so they have options but they just do not see it yet in their future. It is not a reality to them.

I have a friend who went to my high school and made his first real estate investment when he was fourteen years old. He bought a property next to Donner Lake near Truckee, CA for $20,000 and financed it by borrowing from his grandpa. Notice I didn't say his grandpa "gave" him money.

When he was about nineteen he sold it for around $250,000. He has had silver since around twelve years old with much more now and has about twenty-four units as rentals. Almost none of our high school alumni even know he does very well financially.

He lives in a modest house, which he is selling because they are moving to what we call a middle class house. He drives a normal fuel-efficient car and still works for a major corporation making a lower middle class income because he is using it to speed up his retirement. Now that's having an option to work.

Between his wife and him with all the investments their gross income is well over $300,000 a year and growing fast. He wants a certain lifestyle even though if he wanted to he could retire right now at thirty-one and have a better retirement than most people in the United States and it's still growing even after he retires.

Another friend of mine has a very successful father. He is a multi-millionaire commercial real estate investor but you would never know it if you saw him. He has an older Jaguar, F150, and an older BMW Z3. He does own a huge home at Lake Tahoe they invited us to for Fourth of July last year that is amazing. He doesn't act rich, dress rich, or spend rich generally by society's standards and that's why he is rich. He was in the Marines and when he got out he got into commercial real estate and eventually met clients who he invested with and partnered with for many years.

Just get that level of freedom or you will be that guy telling the younger guy when you're sixty to put money into their retirement early because you didn't and you're still working. Don't be a rich person with a job either if you ever come upon it. Make sure you are investing for your future lifestyle that you wish to have.

#18

RICH PEOPLE LOVE JOBS

Do know why this sucks? Because they figured it out before you did. If you can create the job and pay someone else to do it while still having a piece of that income, you my friend are on the right track. A small business is a model to this. Sure, you can make more money by not paying employees, but then you are trading your time which is limited and your business will plateau with no more profits. To get past this step you must hire more people and pay them to increase productivity.

Would you rather make $125,000 a year and work 20 hours a day or make $20,000 a year, hire other management, employees and show up once a week? I chose the latter any day. It gives me time to focus on growing the business, investing, and growing another business. The rich love jobs because if they create them, they are freeing up their own time. Freedom is what we are striving for.

Here is a quick way to look at it. Right now I am building a cabin on one of our properties near Folsom Lake. Now, I can either rent some small equipment for $240 and break these rocks up myself and move them or hire a guy with a tractor for $320 to come do all of that. Well, $80 is worth it to hire out in my case. The equipment I rent may not get the job done the same as a tractor can, and by the time I actually finish I may only have paid myself $5 an hour assuming it works out. I actually dug out four of those holes for my foundation and it took all day long because of the rock I had to break up. I needed 16 of them. Sometimes it's cheaper to pay out.

Another example is if I frame the place myself it may take me awhile to finish although saving some money. The problem is I will have to rent longer as I won't have the cabin done near as fast and I have to pay day care every time I'm out there and that's pushing $1,000 a month! If I can pay $2,000 and have someone help me frame, put the siding on, roof, and get the sub floor together in a week, I'm saving money. Or I even got free labor as I would have spent that in rent and day care before.

I would prefer to pay good workers well at a business I own and focus growing that business or starting another than working myself to death for a better wage. I think the wealthy would agree. They wouldn't have such large businesses without hiring people for jobs that they don't want to do anymore or can't because time is limited.

#19

YOUR BOSS SUCKS

We kind of discussed this in #6-- the people you work with. But we need to elaborate on this one. Whether it's your upper management or the owner of the company, bosses suck. You're like a child at all times subject to their beck and call. The only reason you still work there is you have no better offer and have to pay the bills.

Like a king or your slave master, your only way up in this company is to brown nose, or be the best because your boss knows you have no where else to go. Otherwise you wouldn't be there. They know you're replaceable and know your pay sucks compared to the cost of living. It's like Kevin Spacey in the movie Horrible Bosses. Maybe that's overkill but close enough.

I have had some horrible bosses. Some were actually bad people. I know I am not alone here. As you read the title of this one I'm sure you went into convulsions and were having flashbacks. I mean your pay is already on your mind and now you have this idiot that can take your future earnings away from you at any moment. You have to remain a good employee otherwise they must replace you anyway so you suck it up and drive on. "Hey water boy, you're fired!" Yea, you know that movie. Same deal.

That's you with the carrot on a string pulling the cart, reaching for that promotion you will probably never get and if you do it just solidifies your future in the JOB market, which brings us to #20.

#20

JOBS ARE FORTUNE TELLERS

And fortune tellers suck! The problem with this one is this fortune teller almost NEVER gets it wrong. Allow me to tell you your real financial future. You work a job and make between $25k to $80k a year and will or have for 40-60 plus years. You will have a crappy 401k account like most people do and will end up with less than $100k in it by the time you're 65. You are dreaming of social security in the future to supplement your retirement but it won't be around by the time you get there if you're my age.

You will probably have to move in with your kids or your kids in with you to help provide for the things you all need. Your pension (if you had one) will not exist. And if it does, it will be from a bailout of an inflated currency because your company, municipality, state, and federal government are broke and can't afford to keep you around.

This isn't rocket science so stop dreaming. The odds that you will work a normal job and retire properly are very slim. If you are under the age of 50 right now, you will live in a different financial world than your parents and I mean drastically different.

Working for the government the last four years and seeing the people I work with thinking they are on the right track to retirement because they have a pension and a small retirement plan was depressing. How do you tell them they are in a dream world when they think they are being 'optimistic'? If a word was ever created by the devil it had to be that one. It is the easiest way to sound like you are positive when in reality your numb on the subject that affects your life in a most dramatic way. Don't be that person. I just hope those people have paid off everything they can so their expenses can be covered by a broken pension and a dying social security program.

I know you are down on time, because the government has placed our businesses in a horrible position due to massive regulation implementation and printed so much money that it's hard to live off of one income now days. But you must invest for your family's sake! Unfortunately very few will. Be optimistic but be realistic. Face reality and realize that the pace you're at will be outpaced by government spending. Think about this for awhile.

Get yourself into real estate investing, stocks, options, etc. Write a book that sells. Not like this one because it probably won't. Make something that brings you royalties. You need these types of income. I'm not saying you must become a stock broker but you had better find one that isn't so "optimistic" about the market all the time.

Right now we are on the verge of a massive crash as I write this. The date today is Monday, March 23rd 2015. You remember I said that. In 2008 we had a horrible crash, that never had the opportunity to crash where it needed to due to the Federal Reserve.

The bubble is bigger and will make a much larger ripple when it bursts.

Find these people who knew ahead of time in 2005, 2006, 2007, and latch onto them. Because the same old talking heads are telling you everything is fine. When they said that last time they were dead wrong so stop listening. There are only two answers. They are liars and have an interest in making sure things stay up or they are down right stupid to the subject. They may sound smart, but don't let them sound smart with your money because your fortune at this time doesn't look so great financially. Next time you clock into that crystal ball gaze deep or at least across the break room at the 90 year old guy still working there...

...because *Your Job SUCKS!*

THE DEAL

Before we get onto some important things I want to show you a deal I was working on with zero money out of pocket. It fell apart later and I will tell you why.

This deal was out of state and were seven fourplexes with a total of twenty-eight units. The owner was much older and had owned them for many years with a very large real estate portfolio. I called his agent to get some information and mentioned I would like to buy all of them so I wanted him to send me the profit and loss statements along with the rent rolls for the units.

I was going to offer a little over a million dollars for all the units which was full asking price and the owner said he wold carry (hold a private loan) for qualified buyers. He agreed to hold a note for the down payment at 6% interest with a long term balloon payment, meaning later on whatever I owed when that date came (balloon payment) I had to pay up his portion that was left.

Next I called the bank to make sure they would even loan if there was a private lien on the properties (second position) and sent them the information for the properties along with my personal information to qualify us. Everything looked great as the property had plenty of cash flow to cover everything along with leaving me a decent cash flow for a 100% financed property. The crazy part was for an investment property the bank came back and said they were willing to loan 80% of the purchase price which generally on investments at that time they wanted 25-30% down.

I called back the agent and his seller agreed to hold 20% down as a note in a second position understanding if I defaulted the bank would most likely take the property and he would get nothing from his note. He didn't mind as he knew the cash flow was good and he was already getting 80% in cash from the bank of the purchase price.

This was the great thing about getting a fourplex as the bank considers them commercial loans and bases most of the qualifications off the property's income instead of your own personal income. Now I am about to tie up a property with absolutely zero dollars out of pocket because even the closing costs the owner would finance and I would pay interest on. Then I noticed a problem even the bank missed. And I mean a big problem.

I went over his profit and loss statements again and realized the property only showed $153,000 income for the year prior and $154,000 for the following year. The rent rolls showed on track for just over $200,000 a year which is what the bank was going by and myself included. I pointed it out to the bank then called the agent and everything started to go dark. It became very hard to contact the agent and when I did get a hold of him it sounded like he didn't even want the property listing anymore.

I made sure that he knew if the cash flow was really only $154,000 a year that no bank is going to loan on the asking price he has as there isn't enough income to justify it. The owner would have to drop the price dramatically in order for the cash flow to work. There were only a few answers to this and I believe the answer was he gave me his profit and loss statement he uses for his taxes so it shows far less income as many people there were paying in cash at one of the units where the property manager lived. Meaning he made $50,000 a year tax free if he was collecting the full $200,000 a year.

His property might really make $200,000 a year like the rent rolls show but he has no profit and loss statement to show it. It could also mean there was an extremely high vacancy rate which means people walk on their rental contract and the units are vacant a lot. Or maybe there is a very tough problem with actually collecting rent from the people who lived there. I made sure I told the agent that I did not care what the guy's personal deal was with income tax but I needed the real numbers for the bank otherwise he is stuck 100% owner financing to someone at a lower price or selling all cash.

I could fix vacancy and payment issues if it were just bad management, but I couldn't fix his profit and loss statements. Eventually I had to pass on the deal and it was still for sale eight months later. I called the agent again and asked if he ever got new information as he still had the property listed under his brokerage and he said there is a new manager and he would try to gather anything they could. He called me back saying the information just wasn't well kept so there wasn't any. I explained again he can never sell to a buyer who finances as the bank would take on a huge liability and since he wouldn't come down on price and do 100% finance I couldn't buy.

That's too bad because it would have been a great deal overall for everyone. This is an example of how having no money means nothing if you build a deal. Harder to do and less of them around but the idea is you don't have to wait for a good deal, you can create one before anyone ever sees it.

THE ECONOMICS

This is personally my biggest reason on why jobs suck and by far the most important. Right now we are supposed to be in this economic recovery but it is a lie. This economy in the USA is supported by the Federal Reserve pumping currency through the system with artificially low interest rates. They decide what your interest rate in the short term will be. Not that we are the only country doing it but we are the biggest debtor nation. Talk about fake it till you make it.

Our government tells us that the unemployment rate is under 6% now but that is also a lie or a trick if you will. According the Bureau of Labor Statistics the U3 unemployment rate was 5.5% in March 2015. Except the U3 rate does not include people who are no longer on unemployment, took part time work, or are no longer looking because they can't find a job. The U6 unemployment rate is the rate they rarely announce in the media and it stands at 10.9% in the same month.

The Household Survey from the BLS shows a 62.7% labor force participation rate. That is the lowest since 1978. It has been like this for a few years now as the following chart shows to January 2014.

Something to keep in mind here is that there are women working now as well. These numbers you see in the 40's to 1970, there

weren't many women in the work force compared to men so this number was bound to
rise. But even including them now we are
having a hard time keeping these job numbers up.

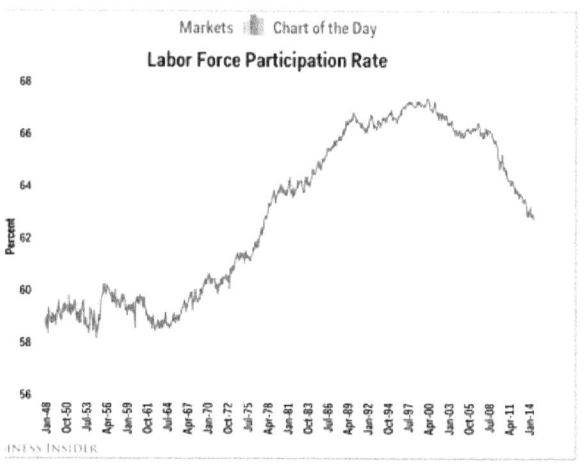

What about the baby boomers? I mean
they are retiring and leaving the workforce
right? I don't think so. According the BLS
statistics the over 55-age group is quickly
taking up all these jobs they are reporting
are being created.

If you are under 24 years old, you are
hurting for a job compared to them. They
are coming out of retirement because their
retirements suck and fixed incomes cannot
keep up with the rising costs of living. The
worst part is these are mostly part time, low
paying jobs. Manufacturing jobs are leaving
this country like the dinosaur because we

cannot compete with Asia if our government is going to regulate and tax our Corporation's profits to death. No wonder they move there, it's not just a currency war.

The April 2015 jobs report just came out so it's the beginning of the second quarter. According to the Challenger Jobs-Cut Report, which grabs mass layoffs from state labor departments, 61,582 Jobs were cut in April 2015. That is the biggest year over year spike for April for 10 years in announced layoffs. The February and March job creation report was revised down as well and their reports were horrible to begin with.

That should scare you for the second quarter because we may produce a negative GDP and the first quarter will most likely be revised down to negative which the wholesale trade numbers show at which point would officially put us in a recession even though I don't think we ever left it. (Update: this was revised down to -.07 which means from December 2014 to April 2015 the economy shrunk 2.9%.)

Except, the FED mentioned recently they wanted to change how they calculate GDP again which basically means they want to cook the books and make it seem as if the economy is growing by manipulating the numbers.

The jobs created were around 223,000 and the consensus was 220,000 with the unemployment rate at 5.4% and they got it!

In fact they called it the "goldilocks" report. Congratulations! But let's take a look under the surface because Wall Street is looking for anything to be excited about. They don't have weather to blame the bad news on at this time or a rising dollar crushing exports right? Now in previous pages I have a chart about people leaving the labor force. Well, I have to add since this is developing as I write this book that we just hit a new record of over 93 million people leaving the labor force.

The Household Survey shows there were 437,000 part time jobs in April and full-time jobs declined by 252,000. Now the government doesn't care to talk about this, they just want the main number because a job is a job right? Now the baby boomers at 55 and older gained 266,000 jobs and the 25-54 age group lost 19,000 jobs.

So again, the numbers show the people who should be retired or retiring are coming back or staying in the labor force and taking part time jobs when the supposed consensus is the unemployment number is going down because these people are retiring.

Don't worry though the FED is going to raise rates according to the market consensus and the FED. The reality is that it's a lie. A bluff like a poker game. The FED's poker face isn't very good but peoples' optimism blinds them from reality. The FED can't raise rates because we would default on our debt and immediately go into a depression.

They are scared to raise it a quarter of a percent. Not to mention what would happen to the housing market. It is the right thing to do but when did any of our central banks care about doing the right thing for the people?

Our economy looks like it's on the light end of a teeter totter but unfortunately it's just uncle FED holding it up because no one is sitting on the other side. I can't even write this book fast enough before the horrible market news comes out. Like the retail sales numbers that just came out. Now like I said, last time they blamed it on the weather, but this time it's April. It was the worst increase in year over year retail sales since 2009, which was the great recession.

How could Wall Street not expect this when prices are rising, consumer debt is rising, and the details in the jobs report lays it all out for them? There is so much wrong with our economy that a bat could blatantly see it. The problem is people really believe the FED is creating a legitimate economy because they catch a headline that is spun. The reality is the FED knows this bubble is too big to pop and if it does, this may actually break the dollar this time around.

Back to the revisions you never hear about. Your employment numbers come out and all you hear on the news is how many jobs were created. They generally fail to mention that they revise these numbers later especially when they are revised downward. For example, here is an excerpt from the March 2015 Non-farm Payroll:

"The change in total nonfarm payroll employment for January was revised from +239,000 to +201,000, and the change for February was revised from +295,000 to +264,000. With these revisions, employment gains in January and February combined were 69,000 less than previously reported."

Things are not as great as we are told. The Fed may be able to pull off QE4 (Quantitative easing. Basically printing money, expanding credit or inflation) and it may work because the market doesn't want to "fight the fed." Unfortunately we aren't the only ones here on earth and other countries can influence our market collapse.

If China started selling their bonds (our debt) on the market it would be like the shadow inventory of foreclosed homes on a bank's balance sheet being liquidated and flooding the market. The bond market would collapse, the only buyer of bonds would be the FED, interest rates would climb out of control and housing would collapse as interest would be far too great to make a payment on a that high dollar loan. This is going to happen unfortunately because the government will not do the right thing. We need our bubble to deflate unobstructed by easy money and face the pain.

It would have been shorter lived if we took

it on in 2001 but Alan Greenspan lowered interest rates which inflated a new bubble in housing and credit. If you think the job market is bad now you just wait. I'm afraid we are in the moment where 2007 has come and gone. The government is saying everything is fine but after the crash they will look back and say January 2015 was the start of the recession.

Look at your money now. The BLS has a CPI inflation calculator where you can type in an amount of money from a past time and see how much it takes today to equal the same value. It says $1,000 in 1950 is equal to $9,739.50 in 2015. That doesn't mean if grandpa saved $1,000 under his mattress it buys you over $9,000 in goods and services. That means it now takes over $9,000 to buy the same goods and services that he would have bought back then for $1,000. His money now can barely buy a nice suit. If he said back then he was going to save it for his grand kid one day and handed it to him in 2015 it wouldn't buy much.

Inflation is a stealth tax eating away at your savings. When inflation is king, savers are losers. Fixed income earners are destroyed and forced back into the labor market. I save in precious metals like silver. I am afraid what is coming is a cashless society. This crash could cause that as the whole world stumbles over their massive amounts of currency they have printed. Most of it is electronic already anyway so it is bound to happen.

Now add this to it. Did you know that there is a stock market crash coming by design? It's the law! Once you turn seventy and a half you will be required to withdraw from accounts that are IRA or Roth IRA, 401k, 457B, profit sharing, and 403B. What happens to the stock market when the baby boomers are withdrawing the minimum amounts? The market will be flooding with shares and prices will fall. Midway through 2016 will be that first mandatory withdrawal for the baby boomers. By 2020 there will be millions forced to take their money out of the market.

THE FINAL WORD

Money is your friend. Maybe your best friend. It never talks back, always hangs out where ever you want to be and it buys you things you want and need. The problem is your job doesn't provide you enough "money friends" to support you and your family in retirement. You need cash flow from real estate, royalties, and stocks. Let's take a look at something.

When you have a job that provides you with $40,000 per year (lets even assume there is no tax) and you buy a $20,000 car, you have spent 50% of your gross income on transportation. Now let's talk about real money. You buy a $500,000 car except you have a billion dollars. Think about this. Ten million dollars is only 1% of a billion. $500,000 goes into a billion 2000 times! That makes it 0.05% of their money to buy a car that is a half million dollars. That is one-tenth of a half of a percent. Doesn't that blow your mind? No wonder the wealthy buy helicopters and planes. Financially, it's like buying a thirty year old Honda Civic with no motor in it.

Try that calculation on our national debt at over 18 trillion. Now do you think we could ever pay it back? Get real. It would take you 32,000 years to count one-trillion seconds. We can only default or have massive inflation and a government will chose inflation every time. I have a 100 trillion dollar bill from Zimbabwe which is a perfect example. There was a hyper inflation there in 2008. This is important because in the last century 55 countries have had hyper-inflation and it is a horrible thing. I have a friend who experienced it first hand in Yugoslavia starting in 1992. Let me list some of the worst ones in our last century.

Hungary: 1945-1946

Zimbabwae 2007-2008

Yugoslavia 1992-1994

Weimar Germany 1919-1923

Greece: 1941-1945

China: 1947-1949

In Germany prices were doubling every 3 days while in Zimbabwe and Hungary it was rated in hours. This is where people are running around with wheelbarrows full of cash that buy you a Popsicle. If you priced gold in terms of the Weimar Germany currency at its peak it was $726,000,000,000 per ounce. Having gold at that time you wouldn't trade it for the hair on your chinny chin chin. You definitely didn't want that currency because everyday it bought you less. This is what is happening right now to your currency as we speak but on a smaller scale. The problem is one day you wake up and all hell breaks loose.

Our national debt as I write this is $18,151,997,679,396. That's over 18 trillion and is growing right now at $45.486 per second. I want this in here so two years from now you can look at that clock again.

Look, I hate jobs so much I even tried to create a license plate that read "YRJOB-SUX" and other variations. The state turned down my purchase and refunded my money because it may "offend" someone. Freedom of speech doesn't go very far with the government. What's funny is I tried so many variations and they were all taken! I appealed and mentioned my book as the reason why and still I was shot down later. The guy at the DMV who I explained my book to thought it was funny because he could relate as his job sucked.

God says in the 4th commandment, six days thou shall labor and do all thy work and the seventh day is the Sabbath and is holy, you shall do no work. But that doesn't mean you have to labor at a job! Maybe you labor in your garden, work on your hot rod, build something, work on investments, a business, skills, or help a friend out. Don't use this excuse because to me it's a cop-out. What do you say when you retire then? We are using society's perspective of labor with that type of thinking.

I have to admit there are a few exceptions I can see to the "your job sucks" idea. Being a pastor, priest, missionary or a nonprofit that actually goes around the world helping people can claim they love what they do even though they are paid to do it. Maybe even saving a life as an emergency room surgeon, fire fighter or certain jobs in the military. Believe me though, there are plenty of people in the military that hate their jobs. I'm sure there is one reading my book right now who thought intelligence was like being in a Hollywood CIA movie but they are sitting in a concrete basement for twelve hours writing reports that the president couldn't care less to read.

When I was a fire fighter I remember going to an accident of a cow verse motorcycle. This guy was messed up and we knew it from the moment we arrived on scene. There was one fire fighter from another agency there doing something outside of his qualifications and later was chewed out for it by the medic at the medi-vac site. I remember him asking me to help with something and I kindly declined and said I would hold the IV bag. Boy I am glad that's all I did. Paralyzed I believe is the last I heard from our captain after he received a call from our agency's attorneys telling us not to answer any questions from outside attorneys should they find us.

This guy's family was trying to sue everyone on scene! So much for helping other people. First responder, law or not, an attorney can ruin your life in a heartbeat. Where's your retirement then? While we are at that subject here is a tip. Don't EVER talk to the police about a crime or incident if you may be a possible suspect. EVER! Always plead the fifth amendment and use that right. Remember this as it may save your life a lot of trouble.

So, again I do admit there are a few but that doesn't mean they don't pay into retirement! They know one day they want to have freedom and have spent their time servicing those in need. Or maybe they want freedom to act more in missionary work or being a marine biologist so they need to buy that freedom to do so. Either way they know retirement is coming one way or another otherwise they wouldn't be paying into one.

I know some things in this book sound crude and <u>de-motivating</u> but think about it like this. People have the notion that motivation is a positive thing we use to move near our goals. But I say motivation is just a vehicle to transport you from A to B. I know this sounds odd but de-motivation is motivation. It literally just has a "de" in front of it.

Think deep for a minute. What do you hear from generally anyone who has became successful that tells their story? Usually it goes something like this. "I was told I would never be anyone, they said I couldn't do it, it was impossible, they said I was a fat disgusting pig, I was bullied," etc. Then what did those people do? They became fitness gurus, millionaires, billionaires, speakers, created amazing inventions and leaders of innovation in our world.

I was one of those people on the receiving end of de-motivation in grade school. I remember the kids not letting me play basketball or football with them at Carlin C. Coppin in fifth grade even though I wasn't bad at it. They just wanted their friends to play. My parents put me in football and boy what a difference. I took all that de-motivation and became the best by my second year. I could play almost every position but mostly I played outside line backer, middle line backer, and fullback. I was also the kicker but I didn't have to stay back because my job was to take people out. I was out there to break you in half by hitting you as hard as I possibly could. Those kids became my friends after that. Eventually I hurt my back multiple times, and I slowed down through high school and eventually went on to motocross and had a few bad crashes there.

I learned it again when I joined the Army National Guard because I wanted to be on an air assault team after 9/11. I had just joined the infantry and was about to get a rude awakening of what that meant when it came to training. I left to Fort Benning, GA the home of the Rangers. Let me tell you this. It was the most demotivating experience of my life and if you are in the military but never joined the infantry in the Marines or Army you have no idea what I am talking about.

Only combat arms like seals, green berets, rangers, and delta can understand and theirs was even harder. You push through and realize that you can go much further than your mind was telling you. Your body is amazing but you quit with your mind first. Looking back I loved the intense training and physical beating you were put through. I was discharged shortly after due that injury to my back in the past.

Without the de-motivation we can argue you may not be the person that they are today or have the same drive. I'm not saying it's OK to do these things, but I am saying that these things created drive. Some people don't use it as fuel and crumble inside. Others rise to the occasion as a leader and challenge the opposition.

You must look at it like David and Goliath. Our military has used this type of motivation for a long time. We call it breaking you down and building you up. So whether you grow up with some great mentor or not it doesn't matter because it's about how you handle your situation and grow from it.

I hope this book helps people understand why jobs suck and to start learning more about investing because times have changed. It's like an old person with a flip phone or that doesn't know how to use a computer. They are left behind as society advances and leaves them on the sidelines while their money is eroded away from inflation and their kids can't pay for their care. Ultimately that was the point of this book. To wake people up and face reality. That it

is time to start your real financial education because 'job security' is not the answer.
Financial security is. Give a man a fish, or
teach a man? That is the question.

Now go fund yourself.

...Buy Your Freedom!

THE END

"Winning"

RECOMMENDED READING

Rich Dad Poor Dad

Along with Rich Dad series of books
- The ABC's of Real Estate Investing
- Tax Advantages of Real Estate
- Guide to investing in Gold and Silver
- Unfair Advantage
- Conspiracy of the Rich

Books by Peter Schiff
- How an Economy Grows and Why it Crashes
- The Real Crash

Book by Edward G. Griffin
- The Creature from Jekyll Island

Book by Ron Paul
- End The Fed

ABOUT THE AUTHOR
Dwight Droze

Dwight grew up in Lincoln, CA before joining the military after high school in 2003 and ending up in Citrus Heights, CA where he continued working for the man. With little money growing up he knew he wanted to be in a different position financially and learned early on in life that working a job until the day you die was not going to be allowed in his future.

He went on his journey learning about the economy before the 2008 crash and what he could do to better his financial future when in 2006 he ran into the book Rich Dad Poor Dad. This was the moment the philosophy started to take hold and answer many of the questions about working your life away.

From this point on he vowed to never settle with trading his time for paper dollars as an employee until the day of retirement. Instead it was time to dig deep and study hard because he never learned this in school and time was marching on. Today he resides in Northern California where his family continues the never ending education process of investing to get out of the rat race.

BIBLIOGRAPHY

- PISA report OECD.org (2012 key findings, United States)

- Pearson Rank and Score—TheLearningCurve.Pearson.com

- March 2015 Non Farm Payroll and Household Survey information—http://www.bls.gov/news.release/archives/empsit_04032015.pdf

- April 2015 NonFarm Payrolls and Household Survey data—http://www.bls.gov/news.release/archives/empsit_05082015.pdf

- April 2015 Jobs cut by ChallengerGray.com—http://www.challengergray.com/press/press-releases/2015-april-job-cut-report-cuts-surge-61582-3-year-high

CONTACT

Dwight Droze

email: bookYJS@gmail.com

www.yourjobsucks.net

twitter@YrJobSucks

www.facebook.com/WhyJobsSuck